Arthur Hall

Who Hath Believed Our Report?

A letter to the editor of the Athenaeum, on some affinities of the Hebrew

language

Arthur Hall

Who Hath Believed Our Report?
A letter to the editor of the Athenaeum, on some affinities of the Hebrew language

ISBN/EAN: 9783337316617

Printed in Europe, USA, Canada, Australia, Japan

Cover: Foto ©ninafisch / pixelio.de

More available books at **www.hansebooks.com**

WHO HATH BELIEVED OUR REPORT?

A LETTER

TO

THE EDITOR OF THE *ATHENÆUM*,

ON SOME

Affinities of the Hebrew Language.

LONDON:

SUTTON, DROWLEY & CO.,

11, LUDGATE HILL, E.C.

1890.

PREFACE.

—◆—

Some three or four years ago, I commenced a close examination of the Hebrew Language, its structure and vocabulary, with the express purpose of detecting all INDO-EUROPEAN affinities open to my research.

When fully completed, I submitted a condensed report of my results to the Editor of the *Athenæum*, who presented the following abstract thereof to his readers, and so to the world at large :—

" Mr. Arthur Hall, of Paternoster Row, is " preparing an elaborate work for publication, in " illustration of his view that all primary Hebrew " roots are identical with Sanskrit; that a good " fourth of the Hebrew vocabulary consists of forms " interchangeable with Greek, while a still larger

A 2

" proportion favor the Latin phonesis ; all being co-
" derivatives from the same Indo-European roots.
" He fancies that considerable light is thus thrown
" on the formation of the Celtic and Teutonic
" branches."

I have reason to suppose that this report, if
noticed at all, was received with general incredulity;
so am led to select for full consideration and
criticism, a few points calculated, as I conceive, to
bring the question thus raised to a final issue.

In now submitting these crude speculations to
public notice, I will only remark that the curious,
and hitherto unnoticed and still *unexplained* coinci-
dences here produced, are but as a grain of desert
sand is to the bulk of the Sphynx there immerged,
compared with the mass of details that I have
garnered for future use.

To the EDITOR of the *Athenæum*.

SIR,

As reference has been made to my labors on the Hebrew roots, I trust that I may feel myself at liberty to address you thus familiarly, and so introduce myself as an occasional correspondent of the *Athenæum*, for a matter of some twenty-five years or so.

I am, Sir,

Yours very faithfully,

ARTHUR HALL,
Citizen and Stationer of London.

CONTENTS.

BERESHITH.

VERBAL INDEX TO No. I.

B—

bai.

Bereshith.

bhu.

boe.

brae, braigh.

brig.

Brigantes.

B'rosheth.

eth.

faurthis.

fore-st, first.

fuerst.

Genesis.

prius, pros, puras.

ras, rasu.

rasoth.

risan, rison.

risc.

rosh.

rosheth.

vi, vo.

I.

BERESHITH.

The Hebrew version of the Old Testament opens with the word *Bereshith*, which has thus given name to the Book of Genesis.

בראשית or *B'Rosheth* reads : "In the beginning," and is, to all appearance, regularly formed according to the grammatical rules inherent in the Hebrew language.

We have the word ראש *rosh*, " head " or " top": Assyrian *rasu*, Arabic *ras*; with the terminal "*eth*," constituting a feminine noun, and the preposition B-, " in beginning," or " in beginning the "; for את *eth* is, by itself a denominative, and survival of the syllabic stage, signifying "it " or " the." *Rosh*, as here used, does not really mean " begin," for, being a noun it is regarded as a derivative, the verb from which it is thus supposititiously derived being lost ; if found, it might resemble the Sanskrit *rish*, " to

llow." But we have ראשון and רישון *rison*, " first "
or " beginning," which compares with the English
word " rise," A.S. *risan*. We have also ראשת
rasoth used for " pillow " or " bolster," which becomes ראשית *rosheth*, " first " or " beginning,"
as in our text.

The backbone of the word consists of the three
consonants " B, R, and S " minus vowels ; if we
substitute P for B, we get the Latin *prius*, the
Greek πρὸς, Sanskrit *puras* ; if we substitute an F we
can manufacture the Gothic *faurθis*, our " forest "
or " first," German *fuerst* ; if we retain the B, we
find the Scottish *brae* so dear to Robert Burns,
Gaelic *braigh*, Welsh *brig*, and so the Brigantes of
Yorkshire. This curious allotment presents the
following problem : Did mankind need all this
elaborate agglutinative process to arrive at the idea
of " first," or was the initial letter born originally
with the word ? In the latter case it will be
manifest that the Hebrew grammarians have
adopted what we call an Aryan root, and chopped
it up to suit their habits.

The prefix B in Hebrew, may be worn down
from the verb בוא *boe*, " to enter " ; I do not pretend

to decide, but it is very curious that in Russian we do find the preposition "vo" which means *in*, and thus exactly equates the Hebrew prefix ב ; yet Russian is certainly a very important member of the Indo-European family of languages, with an exact genealogy.

Boe "to enter" means also "to come" or "go," and I venture to suggest the Sanskrit *vi* or *bhu* as equivalent, either will do phonologically or textually ; and it equates the prefix "bai" in the Greek βαίνω.

I have not undertaken this with any desire to undervalue our Scriptures ; the Bible is a great boon to man, for it has diffused knowledge and civilisation ; true, parts are obscene, so is man ; parts are violent, cruel, predatory, oppressive, so is man ; the better parts will, and do elevate those amenable to its influences, the worse parts serve to attract the baser metal, and thus spread its ultimate influence.

My object is simply to inquire if the irregular grammatical structure of the Hebrew language is any bar to its admission as a member of the Indo-European family of languages.

THE WORD GENESIS AND THE GREEK ZΩON.

II.

THE WORD GENESIS AND THE GREEK ZΩON.

Starting thus with the Book of Genesis, it will be sequential to point out that this word, so familiar to our ears, is directly descended from the Sanskrit root word *jan*, "to beget," Latin *genus*, Greek γένος. The fact is self-evident, and the process has been explained in every authoritative Lexicon, Dictionary and Cyclopædia dealing with Etymology. Sanskrit is a very copious language, and we have vast remains of Hindoo literature from a remote epoch ; it is unquestionably the first, the very earliest mass of erudition known to mankind ; and, while not to be compared with the classics of Greece and Rome, is yet more vital, more accessible than the stone slabs, cylinders and seals of Nineveh and Babylon, or the papyri of Egypt. This Indo-European root *jan* is, I find, equated by the Hebrew זן Zan, a sort, a species ; the Chaldean זון Zun, "to feed," for *food* is

B

the staff of *life ;* from it we obtain the Hebrew מזון *mazon,* " food." But I write more particularly to draw attention to the Hebrew form צאן *tsaon,* used for " a flock " generally, and specifically as a plural for sheep. This last word *tsaon,* I hold to be precisely identical with the Greek word ζῶον, meaning " an animal," " any living creature," yet I do not venture to call it a loan word.

The question is now very complicated, for I find that in Assyrian *sinu* or *tsenu,* which means "good," also serves for " sheep," " goats," etc. ; these two forms, so much alike, are called respectively Assyrian and Babylonian, but they are only dialectical variations of the same form, however applied, and they equate the Arabic *dania.*

I am not aware that anyone has ever yet ventured to compare these old Semitic forms with any living European language, and specialists will hesitate to mix up the Hebrew ז and צ in one etymology ; but I must point out that the Assyrian *Sinu* quoted above closely allies itself with the Hebrew שׂה *Seh* for " Sheep " which, as with us, has no *real* plural in Hebrew.

Nor is it necessary to look to the Hebrew עז *ez,*

" a goat," plural עזים *azim*, for any explanation of
צאן *tsaon*, " a flock " of *goats*, etc. ; this last word,
so far as I can at present see, is more like the
Greek ζῶον than any word that can be produced
from a Semitic source. If however it is not a loan
word, it can only come from the Sanskrit *jan* ;
which also produces the Gothic *Kuni* " a tribe,"
English " kind."

THE NAME OF ITALY.

VERBAL INDEX TO No. III.

Ashtoreth, Astarte.

bath, bathal.

Bethulah.

bhu.

bion.

fitalos.

fui.

Hestia.

Ishtar.

Italy.

phuo.

Sum, f. esse.

ush.

Vesta.

Virgo.

vita.

Vitellius.

Vitulus.

III.

THE NAME OF ITALY.

————

The Hebrew word בת *bath*, for "daughter," begets בתל *bathal*, a "virgin," which becomes a personal name as בתולה Bethulah, the constellation Virgo; it represents some deified female, whether Ishtar, Ashtaroth or Astarte is unimportant, all three words are of identical origin, perhaps from the Sanskrit *ush* "to burn"; but, though their cults were different, they all mean the Queen of Heaven.

The word *Bethulah* compares very closely with the Greek *Fitalós*, Latin *vitulus*, supposed eponym of Italy; the word is explained as meaning a female calf, but I prefer the above suggestion, which plausibly elicits the goddess VESTA, the Greek έστια, a fire deity, whose worship, transferred in early times to Italy, was centralised in her temple at Rome, where the sacred fire was perpe-

tually attended by her vestal acolytes, all *pure virgins*, for this is the point of contact with *bathal*.

If then we compare *bathal* with *Vitulus*, V and B interchanged, we may refer back the Hebrew בת *bath*, to the Sanskrit root *bhu*, " to be," Greek φύω and βίοω, Latin sum, *fui*, esse, " to be," and *vitu* for *Vitellius*, from which also comes our English word *victuals*.

But *vestal* is from the Sanskrit *ush*, " to burn," and it is at this point that the split or separation takes place, for there is nothing in *ush* to suggest virginity, which idea can only come from *bathal*.

No. IV.

THE KESITAH.

VERBAL INDEX TO No. IV.

THE STAR RIGOL.

VERBAL INDEX TO No. V.

agal, agar.

ankulos.

Ares.

Aruna.

Baal.

Hercules.

hora, horaios.

Koh-i-nohr.

Mars.

Nergal.

Nimrod.

Nrigal.

nur, nurru.

Orion.

pramantha.

raj.

regal.

rego.

Regulus.

Rigol.

rijl.

wriggle.

V.

THE STAR RIGOL.

Rigol is a star of the first magnitude in the constellation known as Orion; pictorially this star fits in with the hero's ankle, for one leg is uplifted.

The Hebrew word רגל *regal* means "a foot," Arabic *rijl*, and I suggest a comparison with the English word " wriggle," for it means " to twist," as does the ankle, *cf.* Greek ἀγκύλος. But *rigol* is only a survival, for Orion represents *Nergal*, the Assyrian god of the chase and of war, the European Ἄρης or Mars, the Scriptural Nimrod and also Hercules, for, treating the aspirate " h " as a mere nonentity, we have ῥακλέης, a very near counterpart of *regal*.* In Sanskrit we find the rather equivocal word Nrigal.

Each tongue may have its favourite and plausible

---

* With "regal" *cf.* Regulus or *cor Leonis*, a star of the first magnitude; Latin *rego*, Sanskrit *raj* "to shine."

etymology ; but in that mother tongue common to all civilisation, the same radical letters are found inherent in all forms. I propose, under correction, to explain Nergal as Ner=nar : Assyrian *nurru*, "light," Chaldee נור *nur*, "light," "fire," Hebrew נר *nur*, "a light," "a lamp"; a root word brought home to us in England by the royal *Koh-i-nohr* or "mountain of light," among the crown jewels : *plus* אגר *agar*, *i.e.*, *agal*, "to collect" supposititiously "drops of light," so expressive of this brilliant constellation. But, "to collect fire" suggests a reference to Prometheus, Greek πρὸ-μηδομαι, a provisional substitute for our word providence, *i.e.*, "providing in advance." Prometheus, in mythology, secreted an ethereal spark of heavenly fire to animate mankind. In Sanskrit we find a very early word, *pramantha*, surviving as "stick of fire," and we know that Nimrod is supposed to have founded Nineveh, and is by some regarded as a fire god, having his counterpart in Baal.

As to Orion, I consider it a metathesis of Aruna, naturalised in Greek under ὥρα, ὡραῖος, ὡρίων.

THE PHŒNICIAN BYBLUS.

C

VERBAL INDEX TO No. VI.

VI.

THE PHŒNICIAN BYBLUS.

It is a curious point that the Phœnician town Gebal, so closely connected with the worship of Thammuz or Adonis, is also called Byblus. The town is a sea-port, situated in a hilly district with granitic formation ; the Semitic name is from the Hebrew גבל *gebel*, Arabic *jebel*, now Jubeil, "a hill." Byblus does not mean "a hill," still there is some analogy.

An earlier Byblus was the seat of the papyrus cultivation, in a low-lying, marshy tract of Egypt; the plant, a *cyperus*, is perhaps indigenous. Its root served as food, its material was manufactured into sail-cloth and used as a substitute for leather, while the exported paper constituted a staple trade. We will assume, for purposes of inquiry, that the stone monuments of Egypt preceded the use of papyrus for records, and that the Phœnicians had cultivated a trade with Egypt in carved and engraved monoliths, and monstrous stone sarcophagi. When writing superseded inscriptions, the Phœnicians took up the second trade, and became paper merchants ; so exchanging the granitic Gebal for the softer Byblus, and the Europeans knew them in this way. And I infer that the change was comparatively recent, because the Vulgate adopts both forms ; thus we have Biblians and Giblians in the same version, where the recent English reads Gebalites. Upon this basis alone can we understand the " stone squarers " of an earlier version, meaning quarrymen, who, by the Bible records, proved a numerous and refractory class. But the point I wish to note is, that Byblus and papyrus are interchangeable terms. B=P, R=L, an interesting comparison. Byblus is from the Sanskrit *pa*, " to drink," whence we derive the Latin *bibo* and our *bibulous*, an exact term for the aquatic reed which sups up the fluid like a drunkard. *Pa* also gives us the Greek πάππος, " any soft, downy substance." Still this may be merely speculative, for the main word πάπυρος is called Egyptian.

No. VII.

THE CORYCIAN CAVES.

VERBAL INDEX TO No. VII.

VII.

THE CORYCIAN CAVES.

I must offer an apology for dragging in the above sub-title, for I have really very little to say about the Corycian Caves, but it is the only way properly to introduce the subject I wish to specialise.

The most noted set of these Caves is that in a hill-side above Delphi, a town of Phocis, former seat of the oracle of Apollo, which stood at the foot of Mount Parnassus, near the Castalian Spring. These caves form a stalactitic recess which has been explored in modern times.

The story of the contest between Apollo and the Python has some features analogous to our legend of " St. George and the Dragon." Apollo thus became the Pythian God, and a local temple, instituted in his name, had its body of Priests and

Sibyls, who uttered his oracles or responses to questions addressed by petitioners in his name. The slain monster expired in stenching fumes, and the rotting body gave rise to the name of Python from the verb πύθω, allied to our word "putrid," so πύθειν, Python; this form of argument exposes the fact that the dead monster had no living name intelligible to the Hellenes. Another school adopts the form πυθέσθαι "to inquire," which may explain the Pythian oracles if not the dead serpent.

As to Corycus or Corycian, it appears that the town of Delphi, Homeric Pytho, was originally named Crissa, apparently a mutation of Corycus; there is another Corycian cave at Korghoz in Cilicia, so non-Hellenic; it has its own sacred spring and a legend of the monster Typhon or Typhœus, so a full counterpart to Python. This brings up the Egyptian Pi-Thoum; if the terminal *thoum* equates the Sanskrit *dhuma* "smoke," our own word "fume," there is a plausible analogy between the two monsters and their names; Typhon, the Greek τυφῶν "a whirlwind," is, I contend, identical with Typhoon, Chinese *ta-phung* or "great wind," but this is disputed.

But, the Python? I have to suggest the following Semitic forms : Hebrew פה *peh* "the mouth," so an opening, from פהה *peah*, also פתה *pathah* "to open," so our own "pit," A.S. *pyt*, Latin *puteus* (Vulgate), Greek βόθρος, p = b. The Assyrian forms, older than Hebrew, run : *pataru* and *pitu* "to open," *pu* "a mouth," *putu* "an opening"; if this last word ever reached the Hellenes from some earlier inhabitants of Phocis, it might well serve as a basis whereon to erect the Pythonic superstructure, it would represent an opening in the hill-side, former abode of some sooth-sayer such as the " Witch of Endor." It naturally follows that we have in Hebrew פתן *pethen*, "an asp" or "serpent," פיתם *peethoem*, "a familiar spirit," "a sorcerer." Was the Greek πύθων utilised to produce these allied forms, or are both formed independently from *peh* פה ?

Apollo represents "the sun," "light"; and, when explorers enter deserted caverns they take blazing torches, or, perhaps, magnesium wire ; they light bonfires to expel the foul fiend of darkness, and purify all noxious exhalations. So might Apollo be represented as conquering the works of *darkness*, sole tenant of a pre-historic cave.

But Phocis—take Φώκαινα " the porpoise"; how
suggestive of the fabled Dolphin, the form taken
by Apollo when he brought the Cretan priests to
minister at his fane in Greece, so to become the
Delphi of historic fame. But the famous χορός has
never been fully explained, for our etymologists
fall back on the Welsh cor in Bangor, a word which
cannot be original. Let me refer to the Semitic
חר char, חור chur or chivvar, " a hole "; כר car,
כור coer, " a circular measure," " a hoop," and הרוז
charuz, " rhyme," " harmony," Latin chorus. If
charuz be a loan word from Greek, yet surely חור
and כור will explain the prefix in Corycos; and
then we have חורים churreem, " caverned, a set of
caves."

VERBAL INDEX.

44

Mars,	providence.	seh,
mazon,	pu,	sinn,
	puras,	sum, f. esse,
Nergal,	puteus,	
Nimrod,	putheim,	taphung,
Nrigal,	puthesthai,	thomm,
nur,	putho,	tsaon,
nurru,	puthon,	tsenu,
	putrid,	tuphon,
Orion,	putu,	Typhœus,
	pyt,	Typhon,
pa, pappos,	Pythian,	typhoon,
papyrus,	Pytho,	
pataru,	Python,	ush,
pathah,		
peah,	raj,	Vesta,
peethoem,	Rakleës,	vi,
peh,	ras,	victuals,
pethen,	rasoth,	Virgo,
Phocis,	rasu,	vita,
phokaina,	regal,	Vitellius,
phuo,	rego,	vitulus
pit,	Regulus,	vo,
Pithoum,	Rigol,	
pitu,	rijl,	Wriggle,
pramantha,	risan, rison,	
prius,	risc,	Zan,
promedonai,	rosh, rosheth,	Zoön,
Prometheus,		zun.
pros,	Satrap,	

POSTSCRIPT.

In drawing these few observations to a close, I desire to furnish an outline of the historical aspect of affairs.

i. I am willing to assume that the Septuagint Version of the Old Testament represents the first form in which the scattered records representing the Jewish sacred writings ever appeared as a connected narrative; that it is no mere translation but the actual composition of Greek-speaking Jews, and that Biblical Hebrew was then in a condition quite unintelligible to the literate world of Europe.

ii. That while the LXX. thus served for Greece, Egypt and the dominions of the Seleucidæ, a natural desire grew up for a version accessible to non-Greek-speaking Jews; that the Hebrew idiom was then first committed to writing by Latin-speaking Jews, living under the sway of Rome; who thus unconsciously modified their native tongue.

iii. Starting with the Assyrian Syllabary allied to Zendic and Persian, so like them derived from Sanskrit or its elements, we see the syllabic stage merge into the agglutinative, under the influence of European grammarians, who, while preserving the Semitic construction, yet added their own phonesis in a manner imperceptible to themselves, and, perhaps, quite unintentional.

IN PREPARATION.

ספר השרשים

SEPHER HO-SHARASHIM:

OR

GLEANINGS FROM

Mediæval and Biblical

Hebrew.

FOREWORDS.

NOTHING is more perplexing to the philologist than the mystery of Hebrew roots. Over and over again, the translators of our sacred text are left to hover hopelessly between two opinions on a disputed passage because (1) we have no reliable lexicographical authority for the right use of a particular word, and (2) in this dilemma, no agreement exists as to its derivation, or, as the expression goes, finding its true root; for, on the existing theory, every Hebrew word has its origin in Hebrew.

Appeals are made to the recorded *opinion* of Rabbi Kimchi, circa A.D. 1240 ; or to Rabbi Jonah ; to Onkelos the Targumist, circa A.D. 60; to Jonathan and to the Talmud of Rabbi Asha, A.D. 427; to Moses ben Maimon, ob^{t.} 1204 ; Rabbini Akiba Jarchi, Jalkut, Aben Ezra, &c. Thus we come to Buxtorff, Gesenius and Fürst ; but what if the whole scheme of Hebrew triliterals be fabulous? The present writer, discarding tradition, has ventured to take an entirely independent course, and, comparing established Semitic forms with various Aryan dialects, hopes to cast a new light upon the whole subject.

From the dawn of history, the Jews have been interlocutors with all races of Europe ; their vocabulary, more especially Rabbinic Hebrew, includes much classical Greek and Latin, all being incorporated by supposititious triliterals, shamelessly invented, like our own postulated roots, to naturalise these exotics. It, therefore, becomes a question, has not this system always obtained ?

Recent specialists compare Biblical Hebrew with cuneiform Assyrian, the *Arameeth* of II. Kings xviii. 26 ; but how did this Assyrian or Aramaic first arise ? The writer thinks this point to be, at present, an inexplicable mystery, and hopes that his humble attempt may tend to show the direction in which future inquiry should proceed.